Defective Version 2.0

Poetry and Prose from an Unthinkable Mind

AJ Romano

chipmunkapublishing
the mental health publisher

Published by
Chipmunkapublishing
PO Box 6872
Brentwood
Essex CM13 1ZT
United Kingdom

http://www.chipmunkapublishing.com

Edited by Lesley Kirk

ISBN 978-1-84991-767-4

Chipmunkapublishing gratefully acknowledge the support of Arts Council England.

"No man is an island.
Do not ask for whom the bell tolls!
It tolls for thee..."
- John Donne

This one is for my perspective changers: Mike, Fred, Ryan, Paul, my favorite girls, a Beaver, and a Demi-God.

Introduction-1

Things look differently
when therapy becomes
public domain,
public record…
public perception.

Comprehend please,
the words I wrote in blood
were meant to stay untouched.

I feel obliged to spill
more snippets of soul
          on the page,

giving new meaning to occupational therapy.

Do not misunderstand
          my handstands
available on Amazon—
          I cannot read it.

I live to write,
selling experiences for the Greater Good.

Read me, misguided, mistreated
beaten down and trodden upon,
          read me.

          I am you.

Listen, and choose—absorb
          the white noise,

before ignorance reigns…

Inspiration is dreamy—
a dreary deadening
separation complex

equipped with phobia of the Muse.

She is sneakily silent,
feeling irreverent to immersed emotions
flooding—

a unicycle balance between
said, shown, and unknown;
the hidden rejections
and objectives unfinished,
unpolished, and unrevised.

My self-despise is maddening.

I am not, however,
some ant blanket-begging
like a helpless child.

I fear God,
thereby I fear myself.

“Fear is your only God”,
the Dead Man exclaimed,
Walking his path.

Perspectives-2

The Chill

It feels differently,
perspectives are keys—
demeaning doors,
open, drop invitations;

  uninvited guests surface,
  bringing purposeful,
  unpredictable demons.

No reasoning or rapture;
staring eye to eye
unblinking and unwavering
  can intimidate,
until syndicates and lords
terrorize quadrants
into territorial gang battles
rattling brain into cranium,
  into solid skull.

The head-pounding maddening manic
mess mysteriously appears,
  from time to time,
  still draped in black cape,
  representing all I hate in me.

The perspective swap and flip,
  not disassociating to prevent pain,

but distancing the urge to resist temptation,
  jumping back on the train going nowhere,

pronounced and purposeless…
  a shell.

Anxious Me

Images of anxious me
freely project themselves,
        imprint the memory-foam laden mattress,

shrouded in shadow,
in the mirror behind
        my slowly brightening eyes
every morning.

When these images
run rampant and graceful
races around my healing mind
I find cyclical and clinical
psychological cycles.

        Maybe it's karma,
a neat little circle
        where what goes around,
        does come around.

Being chased by mistakes—
an Elephant Man curse.

In a perfect world,
I would have an answer.
        In a perfect world…

Life

Rising and falling rapids
baffle beautiful abortion—

the abortion of love, of hate,
          not of pain.

The gains are immeasurable,
a bungee jump—

right before you leave you always feel like you are
forgetting something but you cant figure out what it is
until its too late to go back because that would cost
more time you don't have but you regret the whole trip
not going back because at the destination, the price is
never fucking right.

The pain is unbearable,
simple roulette—
because you know betting it all on double zero is fifty to
one odds and you want to get rich quick so you throw
down your chips without thinking it through and soon,
way too soon, *you* are *you* again, and *you* lost.

But it didn't cost chips it cost emotions and devotion and
faceless procrastination fashioned to the highest degree
and purchased Gucci and it felt right but now where are
you?

Lying in the river, floating and fighting rapids
          rocks and leeches;
they bite and hold on for dear life, the same as you.
Time is priceless,
be happy it wasn't the Russian kind.

Something to Think About

Contemplate life without outside
        interference
        interfering
with perception, forcing reality.

Open eyes wide,
        close mouths dripping truth,
        running down your chin—
raindrops are tomorrows forecast.

Where is the box we are supposed to think outside,
        yet get ostracized for doing so?

You play on planet Earth,
        I'm thinking universe;
tiny places in wide spaces
        we think we understand,

lets try and get passed
the kinetics of a working hand
how that came to be
before pretending theories are fact;

        preach Biblical
        Big Bang bullshit,
        preach Darwinian
        idiots eating fruits
        for being hungry,

I would have eaten it too,
        screw the snake,
        an apple is an apple.

Behind the rhetoric,
why look behind?

We are here however we are here,

we are here, living,
        show me how knowing
        how furthers our understanding
of why.

America's 5th Farce to the Constitution

Perception is real—
undefined reality.

I cannot feel
responsible for reactions
        yet they remain judged;

my peers are faceless
        in the jury box.

Judge My Cover

Without claiming to be above ants
of the cosmos,
        (or specks on dirt on Atlas' shoulder)

I can claim experienced-based knowledge
of the collage—
        Picasso inside perception.

Perspective and perception are interlocked,

and society swallowed the key.

        Do you see me?
Do you perceive me?

Egotistical Mania (not devoid of Reason)

Above clouds,
        playing the Sims
        in The Truman Show

means slowing time
to meet needs;

The ruse remains
in exterior-changing ability, at will.

My terms—
        perhaps they enjoy tractor-beam monotony,

I wouldn't know, from up here.

I Stick to Blackjack

Concepts contain information
for impatient people
playing Roulette, .38 at hand—

interpreting information
is introspective and unique.

Ignorance—
inability or unwilling

Id, ego, or superego…?

to use peripheral vision
for peripheral emotions

without ringing out brain cells,
allowing perspective to puddle,
evaporate away.

Wasteful plagiarism
placed here and there,

nonexistent to wise and meaningful.

Not necessarily like-minded,
but maskless without vulnerability.

My Lizard Poem (Ode to Morrison)

Snakes are commonly seen
as vehemently venomous vultures,

ruthless cruel creatures,

grimy, grimacing creatures—

    seen from snake eyes,
    why not wound
    for trespassing
    or baiting,
    or taming,
    or capturing
    or caging?

Shed your skin to layer learn,
    progress with success…

snake.

Love-3

3.1

Normal days and early nights—
	I feel like one of them,
	screamed the dreaming
	sixteen year old,

awakening to warm and damp

thoughts of pleasant fantasies
	dancing,

red lipstick on a mirror.

Other days and other mornings—
wishing Dorothy-winds would take me back;

	an enjoyable reality, unmatched,

wind-swept gleaming,
and always blonde,
	green eyes.

3.2

Does anyone love love?
Truly, many like love,
enjoy draining endless emptiness,

        being wanted
        public image
        sex sex sex
        or money,

liking love is appealing;
a break from dreary dreams
and isolation. Meaningless.
Empty.

Loving love?—
True,
        a migraine packing explosives,
        McVeigh's truck
        traveling on the interstate
        connecting neurons
        spinning out of control

until they have illuminated
        or eliminated all that existed,
and you are one,
a healthy hybrid
        living in healthy hyperspace.
Much more vague,
        loving love,
        ambiguity.

I chuckle at the rising divorce rate,
        contemplating my fate,

knowing I hate liking love.
        And loving it.

3.3

Renewed love is miles above new love;
gliding free and clear, thirty-thousand feet—
cruising altitude, no turbulence,
no fortitude necessary for a casual traveler.

Business class, first, or coach?
        Irrelevant to her relevance;
        to her elegance, compassionate
        passion only her glance can explain.

It rises not outside but inside,
sure as the tide, overwhelming and welcome,
        not destructive;
clear, quiet and aquamarine diamonds lapping the shore,
brilliant in the moonlight—the glints of her eyes scanning
mine,

interpreting secret signals
        no Patriot Act can interfere with,
        no evil glare attack,
but love in its purest form,

unique and challenging,
warm and comforting,
until you can't let go—

the feel of her heart beat intoxicating,
        a persisting and addicting drug
        no meetings or steps cure;
a welcome disease.

A disease always meant to please,
        love is all you need.

I found what I need John,
        it was more than I ever "imagined",
I am alive.
        And aware.

3.4

I feel it creeping again,
    the Reaper named numbness,
a lack of progress and success
    futile from your fake face,
    lies flew from fake eyes,

I should have seen deceit
    through your teeth
    but diluted by my polluted
    delusions of amusement
    and feelings of feelings
I never felt,

but was fucking certain
    I would burn
    betrayal for portrayal of feelings

I could not stop reeling
    and reeling and reeling
until I lost the line and track of time,

blindsided,
    a fucking deer in the headlights
    staring scary spaces in the face,
    knowing surmise meant demise.

And it did.

3.5

The fascination lies in the creation—
gateways marked by Peter,
        scarred;

        one-night-stand crack rocks
        demean meaning in the climax climb;
the yellow brick road to happiness
without a glass ceiling or wizard
on the other side.

Magic is alive in eyes;
no wand or spells or Hogwarts
needed to spark the powder keg
        demolishing marks and Peter's scars,
replacing them with the fancier dancer of grandeur,

the fancier dancer of bliss and happiness
getting stronger kiss by kiss,
glance by glance;

mind dances turn to Tangos
and romantic red roses,

without thorns to bore holes,
but sweet sap to scour scars
        and empower victims everywhere.

Isolation is making me sick;
limp walking, crippling a crippled downgrade,
        downgraded and frustrated,

until I'm face down
skewed, mind-whipped
        with exploding methane,
        and unwelcome, morning migraines.

I numb myself again;
we're back to best buddies,

until I wake up face up
ceiling-staring
teeth-baring
and nails tearing
every inch of skin I can find...

I realize I'm in my mind,
facing what I try to hide.

Do you expect me to be cynical?

3.6

Looking at love objectively,
        partially uninterested—

human beings see presentation
as materialism;
        mutually exclusive to be truthful.

Produce a situation to prove
devotion matters more
        than instant retinal eye-flashes
        and interpretation of said flashes—

We are unique, monotonous flash-cards.

        Lucy, I'm home.

Rinse, repeat.

3.7

You must love to be
loved.

You may remain unloved,
        inappropriate
        and inadequate
as it seems—open hearts are steam burns…

water is necessary,
        when your lungs fill to the brim and spill
        organs out of your mouth

        or when it boils and you need your coffee so you rush
        to obtain your craving…
you may learn, that which sustains us

        can set us free.

Drown, or burn in love…
        I'll ask Alice.

3.8

Inabilty to obtain emotional attachment
detaches me more every day

from every day—
conversations and interactions
are distraught distractions
because plowed fields are golden from above…

ground level looks lonely and yellow,

and empty.

****

We spoke,
        blindsided, slapped and stunned.

I was knee-bound, praying,
        without words.

Silence—
        comfortable understanding
        demands undue attention!

Clicked and connected,
bonds without bondage,

filled brim tight with compassion.

        A ball in playground unknown circles the rim—
        a buzzer heart beat beating,
ranting, craving a future,

with dust behind to divide mistakes.

Do I *love* her?
        (Yes).

Tragedy-4

(the following stories are fictional, but situational. I am everyone you love to hate)

Together we will stare grief in the eyes—
different kinds of grief:
    lying and hiding,
    binding and tying,
    and upfront and crying.

The details are important,
you see, they will be,
    they can be

the worst piece to the puzzle,
    whether it fits or not.

To make it fit, or to
accept the unacceptable?

It Has Been Ten Years...

Let me start by telling you about the day that ended my life forever. It was a crisp post-summer day, warm enough for a t-shirt, but cool enough for a pair of jeans, Beautiful day, God-awfully beautiful. I remember it; our alarm went off at 6, as usual.

I hit snooze, as usual.

This day, today *was* different. I crept out of bed quietly as a child sneaking a midnight snack, and headed for the hard wood of the stairs. The wood was cold, I remember, but I was careful not to start, careful not to make a sound. I knew that today was the beginning of the rest of my life.

She must have heard the crackling of the bacon grease on the frying pan, or perhaps it was the smell of the freshly ground coffee that woke her, but in any case she surprised me in the kitchen.

“Why didn’t you wake me, love?”

“Breakfast in bed *would have been* a wonderful surprise, but, thanks to you, it’s ruined. Thanks Anne, I appreciate it. I appreciate you waking up today. Now you get clean-up duty. Ha.”

She giggled at my sarcasm. She had a love/hate relationship with my sarcasm, which was abundant. She frequently commented on how weak people use sarcasm to take the attention off their weaknesses, yet she always seemed to find humor in it. She was that kind of girl, I guess.

“What is on the agenda for today?” I asked simply. I always found her work fascinating.

"Well, I have a meeting at 8:30 with the partners, you know, to explain that proposal I was telling you about. This could be it Jim, it really could. This time tomorrow I could be on the other side of the table, taking proposals from the peons rather than giving them, as one myself."

She always put herself down. But she was real.

"You've been working on this forever, how could it be anything but perfect? I know you will blow them away. And if you don't, fuck 'em, right?"

"No, Jim, not 'fuck 'em'. These people are my bosses; I have to care how they feel."

"Anne, be realistic. These old maggots will be dead or retired in the next five years. You have worked your way up in that company from the ground up; they need someone like you. They need someone who knows their company, inside and out. You will blow the fake hair right off their heads, I promise you."

"I hope your right..."

"I am right. Nothing short of a bomb going off will ruin this for you, honey."

The world is sarcastic too, I suppose...

We took the train in, together, just like every other day. New Jersey is certainly not the prettiest state in the Union, but something about that day was simply splendid, unreal even. The landscape seemed to fly by too quickly, too smoothly. If you live in Jersey, and you have taken the train into the city, you understand landscape to mean traffic on the Turnpike, a glimpse of Newark Airport, and the ever-famous Secaucus

Junction, the two million dollar train station that nobody ever uses.

Her head rested on the shoulder of my blue maintenance jacket, which clashed horribly with her grey, formal, pants suit. It was almost unrealistic that we worked in the same country, much less the same building. It was even more mind blowing that she was content with a working stiff like myself, not some Park Avenue douche bag. But I was a writer, and she understood that. I was just making ends meet. I was not going to get stuck working in that basement forever, and I was sure of that.

How right I was.

Today, we were running a bit late. Breakfast cleanup took a little longer than expected, I suppose, but those details are long forgotten and ungodly irrelevant. An older gentleman in a business suit gave up his seat on the subway for her; I remember that like it was yesterday. It made me quickly contemplate modern society, and what we have turned into. This man, who, quite honestly looked in his seventies, gave up his seat for a young lady, because that is the way he was raised.

My parents raised me that way, I thought, but I knew I was in the minority. Maybe that *is* what she saw in me, simple decency. That simple act of kindness was enough to make me silently thank the man by taking him by the hand and helping him onto the platform. He understood. Perhaps decent minds are as alike as great minds.

The business district was hustle and bustle as ever. The closer we got to the Towers, the faster the pace became. I remember thinking about these men and what they did. I laughed out loud.

"What's so funny?"

"Look at them, all of them. Imagine what they look like from God's perspective." I was by no means a religious man.

"What do you mean?"

"Buy, sell, buy, sell, buy, and sell. They are doing nothing but playing Monopoly with other people's money! And not that cheesy McDonald's online monopoly, the real game."

"I never liked that game, it takes too long."

"A lifetime, my love, a fucking lifetime. But these people don't really care, do they? Like I said, it's not their money. They might as well have just pulled it out of the box, and stamped it like the Treasury Department. Little pieces of paper control everything."

"Money doesn't control me!"

"Sweetie, if it did, you certainly would NOT be with me." We approached Tower One. "Now get up there, and show those old bastards how brilliant I KNOW you are."

She smiled and gazed into my eyes. I smiled because she smiled. My thoughts left New York, and traveled back home, to the engagement ring tucked safely in my lock box under my bed.

Even though I had been awake for a few hours, I was still somewhat bleary-eyed. I never was a morning person; she truly was my reason for waking up. I went about my day-to-day business for her, and only her.

At age sixteen, I was diagnosed as Bipolar I. I have struggled for years with the disease; medication to doctor, to medication to inpatient treatment, to medication to more doctors. By the time I hit twenty I was on more medication than most eighty-year old women I knew, and this eventually culminated into a serious psychiatric breakdown. I wanted to leave. I needed to get out of the 1950's suburbia I felt like I was falling into. My nuclear life was bent and broken, and simple monotony was simply maddening, until I met her.

It was her smile, I think, that did it. The smile that made me smile; the smile that could end wars; silence even the most obnoxious of our kind, and pick all up from the ashes. The smile that was medication; I fed off her happiness. She pulled me, a psychopathic aspiring writer with no prospect other than self-projected, out of the dank, dark hallway with no end.

I stood up. I got a job, meaningless though it was. It was stability, and she was my foundation. I could no longer relate to Atlas, the burden was gone. It was just Anne, and, at the end of the day, it was always just Anne.

I asked her, one day, why she let me buy her that drink. She asked me why I bought it to begin with. There was no winning these battles; she was my intellectual equal.

"Your eyes," she finally responded, "You had the most beautiful eyes. I could tell, right there you know, with eyes like that, how could I go wrong?"

She always knew how to get to me.

This is what got me through the day, thoughts of serenity and thoughts of Anne. Thoughts of beginning the cycle again, white picket fence and all. Maybe a dog too…neither of us were cat people.

Like I said, I was still bleary-eyed. I only had one cup of coffee, and trust me, it was no Starbucks. So when the blast knocked me off my feet and into the concrete wall of the second basement sublevel of Tower One, I couldn't tell you whether I had been punched or simply fallen asleep standing up.

I came too quickly. Something was not right. I quickly took in my surroundings. I heard screams from above. I could see nobody around me, yet I sensed a presence. The taste of iron was repulsive, and it wasn't until I reached for my throbbing head that I realized I was bleeding rather steadily. But that did not matter. I moved for the elevator, but thought better of it.

I had no idea the horrors I was to find when I ran up those two flights of stairs. I looked at the clock. 8:49. She was in the main conference room on the 108th floor. I hit the lobby and expected to find some semblance of order, some semblance of familiarity. All I found was panic. There was nobody to ask, nobody to speak to, nobody to relate with. There was, instead, a herd of cattle headed for the door, not one looking back. It was like they were headed out to slaughter, ignorant of what lie ahead. It was raining from the ceiling, as apparently the fire alarms were going off. All I could hear was sirens. They reverberate in my brain to this very day; they are the last thing I hear before I fall asleep, and the first thing I hear when I wake up.

Getting to her would be impossible, I thought. I tried the staircase, more than willing to run up a hundred floors. The mob was impossible. I exited the building to assess the situation. She is probably already evacuated anyway.

The outside was no more familiar. I had stepped into Beirut. The blaring sirens hit me again. Blaring, blaring, and incessantly blaring. I was not prepared for what I was about to see. I looked up with everyone else, feeling like a duck in the rain, mouth open, ready to drown.

When I saw what had happened, I was floored. I froze. One of the three jewels of the famed New York skyline had a gaping hole in it. Fires blazed like Dante, I could feel the heat from the ground level. The 108th floor! I guessed that a bomb had gone off, probably around floor 90. Anne. Floor 108!

I moved so fast the building seemed to be running towards me as well. I had to get back. Another unexpected blow and I was thrown to the ground again. I was being dragged away by a firefighter or a police officer; at the time I saw nothing but a uniform. Mania kicked in. He told me the building was being evacuated. I told him her floor. The look on his face was a response enough. I was back in that hallway, dank and dark as ever.

And then it happened, and it all seemingly made sense. At 9:03, I witnessed a plane crash into the South Tower. I saw it; I saw the nose of the plane go in one side, and come out the other, in nothing but shambles. At the same time I saw the looks on the faces of every passenger, the pilot, and Anne. It was the same look we all had, Horrified, yet resolute, Scared, confused, yet seemingly expectant. We all knew there was no happy ending this time, we all knew.

That moment I saw the look on every mother's face, I saw the tears well up in their eyes as they told their eleven and twelve year olds that we were now at war.

War Such an archaic word to a child growing up in the 80's and 90's. School teaches us World War I was the war to end all wars. World War II was a result of Hitler's rise to power, and the Japanese attack on Pearl Harbor. But these were military wars, fought far from America's heartland. The World Trade Center was no military target, and Anne was no soldier. We knew we were at war then. We just didn't know with whom.

I did what I could. I helped the elderly move away from the towers. I shielded the eyes of the children from the horrors above. I assured the women that their husbands were fine. The fires would be out soon, and Anne would walk out the door, she would see me and she would smile. She would smile and I would smile and it would all be okay. This is truly the delusion that I created; the delusion that kept me going as an able bodied man, a decent man, a man not helping because he has to, but because he was thrown in a situation that forced him to react. Decent people react decently.

I was barely able to speak when the South Tower collapsed. All those people those innocent working people. All the way from the bankers and lawyers in their business best, to the maintenance and mail-room workers making ends meet. Gone, buried, and gone. Mothers, fathers, grandmothers, grandfathers, children, aunts, uncles, and cousins were buried amongst the steel and concrete. We are all the same.

Deep down, we all knew what was next. 108th floor! I saw the bodies falling from heaven; they had given up hope. They didn't want to burn, no ashes to ashes for them. Fuck 'em. Isn't that what I said to her? Fuck 'em. They aren't going to take me! I'm going on my own terms, culminating in a glorious free fall.

My life ended on September 11th, 2001 at 10:28am. The skyline cried for its fallen twins.

I was broken, again.

Ushered in by parades
of bombs and falling towers
and chaos,

we follow the leader off the cliff,
into civil unrest;

rebellion swells swollen bellies
starving for change,
craving its success
and lack of death.

Potential poison joins ranks
with death at the river's edge,
collecting death-price and love-toll;

pay the man and move on,
or chance fond memories—
a future glance unpredictable,
not unreliable, but inspired
by tireless grinding at the stone,

creating beauty; unmatched,
dispatched and shimmering,
sharp, spiked, and hazardous
for the novice handler.

The money-man means business—
distress or the best confession
means nothing; no comfort
by experts or otherwise;

the prize is not selling your soul
        but giving it, willingly, happily,
        and guilt-free.

Pride means nothing on the ride of love—
        a vile, made-up emotion; devotion is real.

Take a chance at romance;
dance in the rain and get soaked
and sopping wet, dripping droplets
of cleansing cold,

her body heat will meet your body heat and you will fall;

not down, but up,
        higher than the highest cloud
        yet more grounded
        than when you lit your first smoke,
        thinking you would get away free and clear.

        This time you may.
Most times you don't.
        Jim didn't.

The Root of the Problem

Jack, glancing into the egg-shell eyes of his distinctive partner-in-crime, and his nearly-distinctive love, says, "I have something to tell you..."

His companion, elated, responded with, "Jesus, Jack I have something to tell you, too! Me first, "she ended playfully and seductively.

Jack contemplated to himself, in a manner of milliseconds. His desire and want for her, and his love for her took over. He has known love was limited since he was a child, Jack has.

Jack's father was a preacher and a mother-fucking hypocrite. He spent all the time he wasn't spending in "confession" with the wife of this congregation members' wife, or that, swilling old bottles of Jim Beam that littered the bottom of his bed until the day he died. Mom took the brunt of most of those drunken-nights, but Jack frequently got in the way as well. So did his sister, Jill...

He had trouble, Jack did, understanding what demon would jump out of the Bible and possess his father to do these terrible things. He would watch his father preach every Sunday from close-by; he would watch the love of God and masked compassion emanate and radiate towards the crowd, rapt at attention, feeling that a loud breath would unleash the wrath of the Maker.

The official report on the death of Jack's father was accidental. He was drunk, stumbling around the kitchen looking for food, wielding a kitchen knife. The alcohol killed him, in the end, said the nice Police

Officer, when Jack's father lost his balance and fell, the knife ending up in his heart...

All Jack remembers was the fight; the image of his father's brawn cocked back, his mother pinned against the flowered wallpaper. Jack opened the door....and blackness. He knows now what happened; his mother, dear Mother, was a quick-thinker. Jack left that town as soon as he could.

Jack made something of himself, perhaps to be nothing like his father. Jack graduated the University of State top of the class, and was now a successful businessman before age thirty, and now had a companion he adored. Jack was the American dream.

Jack was now patiently awaiting the obviously stunning news he was about to receive, from his stunning companion.

"Listen, my love [her smile melts Jack's soul, even today], I have been thinking about...well the *question* ["oh, no, not this, not this for her, not this right now...should I stop her, can I stop her, I know...it's best...I already killed once...", Jack thought, remaining resolute] you asked me, and...well, MY ANSWER IS YES, LETS GET MARRIED!"

His mind was made up.

"I am sorry you went first. My news was the complete opposite. I must leave, and now. You cannot come with me, I am sorry, but I do not love you. I don't. Goodbye."

Jack ran as far away as he could, and as fast. He left his companion standing there, dumbfounded and crying, in his own posh apartment, and never looked back.

He checked himself into a hospital a few states away, famished.

Jack died a week later from the late-stage Pancreatic Cancer he chose not to tell his companion about.

Six-months later, his companion gave birth to a boy.

It was his.

The moral of this story—
honest, clearly true,
        but a mirror after a hot shower,
        a masquerade with a smoke machine.

Jack rose, Jack fell—
        his companion left with a puzzle missing pieces.
Perhaps pieces to a different puzzle…

        It is a wonder,
        six-feet under,
        because dying
        cannot be lying.

Did my homework,
or my cat ate it,
the check is in the mail, sir,
and *you are* getting a deal,
        baby, I promise I won't…

Dying is honest and wholesome,
not sorrowful, not shameful;
        certainly not dignifying.

The dead are dignified,
        immune from the lies and pain of this existence.

Lying is not always lying,
they remain at peace.

The question is not "why",
        it never can tie the worlds
        dividing the human race.

Look at the "what",
        and occasionally the "what if"…

What if the companion watched Jack waste away for weeks,
pressuring her and pressuring her,
knowing her child will be fatherless
and knowing they were "making him comfortable"
and knowing she would watch the light leave his eyes
and her last memories would be wiping the drool
off his scrawny, wasted chin.

And then she miscarried.
What if?

Masochism's Function

Please do not confuse Jim with Jim,
though they could be the same,
I suppose, in a different dimension...

For all intents and purposes, this *is* where it begins. My life, I mean. We are talking like Sylvia Plathe begin, not the whole science/religion bloody placenta bullshit where Mommy can cry, and Daddy can either revel in self-loathing or make a bee-line towards the nearest garbage can to prove that he had been surviving on Snickers bars and cheap coffee for the past few hours. No, not that begin.

I suppose Sylvia Plathe is not the best example, as she was more concerned with the eternal process of dying, rather than the short time we, as humans, are actually living. I mean really, our lives in the *globalized* world we have created are really more defined by the cars we drive, the size of our flat-screen LCD's, the amount of Xbox's in our houses and the like. It's nothing more than a new-age "keeping up with the Jones'" with the subtle, yet crucially important difference that now we really can shove a nuke through your suburban living-room picture window from thousands of miles away, and, no, screaming FLASH and hiding under a fucking school desk will not make two-shits of a difference.

You can call me a cynic, really, I don't mind. I suppose I am, in the bare-bones definition of the word. Just do me one favor, hear me out before you judge; most people like me would have a dozen kills under their belt by now, notching off lives like writing off expenses on a tax report.

I could get into the grisly details—child abuse and abuse and abuse, alcohol-fueled rage, and then love, and then rage, choosing foster homes with a blindfold and a dart board (pin the tail on the failure). That, however, is wholly irrelevant, or at least I thought it was, which most of the problem is probably to begin with. Blind acceptance is not acceptance; it creates, in the words of Sir Paul, “a face that she leaves in a jar by the door”.

Fitting in was a joke, really, too easy to comprehend, too easy to fool everyone else, which is probably why I didn’t bother trying. When the then-high school-gods-of-football-later-gas station-attendants (when they realized that “throw a football 50 yards” has no place on a job resume) would extend a friendly blessing of an invitation to one of their “epic” parties, I would mostly oblige. It was mutually beneficial; I could drink until the point of obliteration, and they could smoke my weed. However, as far as I can remember, I was never one of them. I vowed to never be one of them. So I sold them weed, the great equalizer.

As an aside, it seems an ironic critique on my part to “look down” on the simple gas station attendant. They get up every day with a cup of black coffee and a cigarette, like me, go about their every day duties, like me, and eventually curl up in bed to wake up and do it again, like me. They however, have freedom to choose which gas station to work at. I unfortunately do not have that liberty; but that’s neither here nor there.

The weekends were actually the hardest part for me, in my younger days, *the void* between mundane reality and more mundane reality. That reality helped fill the void though; in school I could sleep off math class to look forward to Chaucer or Shakespeare, or even making a new piece to burn the token green stuff out of a test tube and Bunsen burner in science class. Once I lit a desk on fire because I was bored. Result: fifteen-minute detention. My lord, the consequences one must face!

It is more interesting, I think, to look at *how* I have gotten to where I am, rather than *why*. Am I a "sociological-product-of-my-environment"? I am, just as much as the inner city forgotten minority who robbed liquor store because Uncle Sam denied his mother welfare and she wasn't educated enough to USE A FUCKING CONDOM in the first place to avoid her entire situation. Bias will be what bias is. I am not bitching, and she shouldn't either. Now her son is in the system and she doesn't have to pay for him anymore, until she has another one. Again, no judgment passed: in the suburbs it gets swept under the rug, or aborted.

The *how* though, that really is the amusing part. I have been called "crazy", or, I believe the term for Gen-X and Y's school children is *emotionally disturbed*. That is sort of broad though, not for nothing. By the classification, Attention-Deficit is considered *emotionally disturbed*. Just give the fucking kid a Ritalin and stop making classifications, please. It will make the kid's zombies (no different than anyone else, really) and the parents less likely to beat the shit out of their kids for not being the star-fucking-quarterback. And it comes full circle, the American dream is realized, the pill bottle and the belt.

I, however, probably could have benefitted from more than some Ritalin, in retrospect. I just found out at an earlier age what most cannot master until much later in life. I found out how to pretend. This may seem a tad, ah, contradictory (?) to my previous statements regarding my childhood behavior, but I am no longer speaking regarding my peers. I mean, for instance, when Billy Hartman called me a "gay-motherless-piece of shit who enjoys taking it in the ass from his fake father" and the hall monitor found him lying in the bathroom, teeth missing, nose broken, pants-less with a pencil shoved up his ass (and me having left the scene of the crime a few minutes earlier, hiding my bloody hands in my pockets) there had to be a sex offender who had just escaped from the window seconds before, right? After they wired his jaw back together, that *is* what he told the police, after all. Billy learned his lesson, and I walked away, smirking on the inside. Who likes it in the ass now, Billy?

I think they made an arrest a few days later; some poor schmuck who got fucked in his ass too, only this time by Megan's Law (and probably by a large Aryan in prison too, as I hear they are none-too-kind to child molesters in Gen-Pop).

That is a metaphor of sorts, don't you see? Hidden blood for hidden acts! Manipulation makes the world go 'round, not money. I mean money can sometimes be effective *in* manipulation, however money is not something I was ever graced with; therefore alas, we are where we are.

Moving past little Billy Hartman (the dude was like 6'3), who, by the way, averted eyes every time he laid eyes on me after the, let's call it *incident* (even now I have trouble admitting I probably just made another such as myself), I was introspective and intelligent enough to realize how close of a call it really was. I certainly was not ready, nor willing, to spend the rest of my "childhood" staring at metal bars and eating with plastic forks, or in a padded room in a pair of cloth, full-body handcuffs waiting for Nurse Ratched to scream "medication time!" in a shrill, and utterly annoying howl. I needed out as soon as humanly possible, and, therefore, decided a partial scholarship and some financial aid was something I could deal with.

College really was utterly wonderful at first. Who would *not* want to live in a place where "drugs, sex, and rock-and-roll" were just a doorstep away? It was essentially an inner-city project for rich white people, affirmative action cases, and those lucky enough to receive scholarships or financial aid (minus the starvation, guns, abandoned children, and extremely loud and obnoxious "hip-hop"). Class was an afterthought really.

What's that? You offer a liberal arts major where I can essentially study whatever I feel like it for four or five years and then get a job doing something completely unrelated to anything I have studied? This is too good to be true.

I am not quite sure whether college is a good idea, or a clever ruse for the masses. You may be skeptical, just throw the idea around a bit. I mean look at it logically; Thomas Jefferson or even Benjamin Franklin, who are men that we base our lives on EVERY SINGLE DAY had no more than an extensive library. No piece of paper that showed them their worth or proved to anyone how "intelligent" they were even existed. And they founded a fucking country. A country! Hey Dubya, shove Harvard and Yale right up your Skull and Bones toting ass.

I think the college idea is so appealing to so many for the same reason our country was founded. Which, in essence, is the same reason our country has become a so-called "melting pot". And again, the same reason the psychedelic-sixties idea of "dropping out" and driving across the country in a piece-of-shit van with no air-conditioning was appealing. It is a new start. When you get to college, sure you are still *you*, but you no longer have to be the *you* that YOU would rather not be. People have no preconceived notions, no family history and no social constraint.

The brand of jeans you wear or the purse you carry becomes wholly irrelevant when you wake up hung over and then smoke a joint to take away the hangover and then realize you are late for class so maybe you brush your teeth before you stop in the pay-caf to grab a cup of burnt black coffee before you realize you are still in your pajamas and probably still smell like weed but when you walk into class you take a deep breath, because you are staring at a classroom filled with YOUs. And acceptance, not perception, is the true reality.

That, right there, hit the nail on the head for me. My whole life I was different, in some sense; the dark, brilliant kid who actually paid attention in English class and corrected the bitchy Algebra teacher with the yardstick on her grammar, while staring out the window and contemplating nuclear holocaust. I was no longer the outcast and it was wonderful, but boring, wonderfully boring. The early bird may get the worm, but the lazy, bored (and somewhat more intelligent) bird knocks the other son of a bitch who took his worm the fuck out of his tree. Again, we come full circle.

I was surviving on the college diet; pizzas, beer, weed, and black, burnt coffee. I have always been a coffee person, and consider myself somewhat of a connoisseur. A good cup of coffee is hard to come by, especially these days. Long ago (long in some sense, anyway), I remember the commercial with the Colombian dude, who was probably just a Mexican with a stupid hat on, talking about his different roasts and how amazing they were if you bought his coffee maker and paid massive amounts of money each month to keep up the deliciousness. Another clever ruse for the rich and famous too drugged up on diet pills to sleep and rely on late-night infomercials to fill *their* void. If you call within the next fifteen minutes, we will double the order, ABSOLUTELY FREE! What a fucking deal, I'll put it right on the credit card I will never pay off because I'll be bankrupt before I get the bill! Me, I'll take a Starbucks Pike Place any day.

Anyway, where was I? Ahh the diet, right; well it was like everything else, really, good while it lasted, but never as sweet as it seems. Things get old, man, everything gets so fucking old. And, really, when they get too old, that's when things get problematic; Problematic for me and therefore problematic in general. Another metaphor.

There was one part of college I had not foreseen the consequences of, the social interaction necessary when living with *other people*. It was easy to control virtually ANYTHING when, at the end of the day I could sit back, alone, and smoke a joint. Just simply smoke to oblivion, maybe pop a benzo or two, and contemplate life. Or not contemplate anything, just be myself. Just be what I believe I should be. This was when I realized that just because people do the same things, day after day, or look the same, or even act the same, does NOT make them the same. Zombified monotony makes this world hell, makes the Inferno look like knocking off an old woman at an ATM devoid of cameras.

I started to notice myself falling into the age-old trap of *conformity*. I don't mean to sound like a sixteen-year-old rebellious goth kid who does heroin to NOT fit in with society, but I suppose it is the same thing. I was not content with living in a place full of people who were actively trying to be as dissimilar as I was naturally. It was maddening to think that when Thanksgiving break came these same kids who, not a few days earlier, were snorting coke off their Business Law books were sitting around the table with caring relatives debating Che Guevara with Grandpa-World War II or Uncle Vietnam. Don't get me wrong, my lack of a family life was not too bothersome; I had nobody to pretend to and this made me rather carefree. I answered to myself. I was simply annoyed that, in my mind, these people strove to be what I already was. But they wanted it both ways, something I could never comprehend.

I eventually turned to isolation, pure and simple. I always found solace in solitude; however, isolation and solitude are two vastly different things. The best way to describe the difference is through Thoreau and Dickinson, really. *Walden* is really the epitome of solitude, an extremely introspective man contemplating thoughts alone in the woods. Dickinson defines isolation from the world as anxiety for anxiety's sake. I began to relate.

I had always been a fan of benzos; Xanax, Valium, and Klonipin played a large part in my *lack* of a mental break to this point, so they seemed a logical place to begin reinventing myself. They made me social, and rather *normal*. That word, normal, is really rather novel. It has been used in so many different ways and so many different contexts it is really maddening. A President, an *American* President (I use italics for the sake of emphasizing American "omniscience"), gave the word a new form of tense for Christ's sake! No, people, "normalcy" was not a word. I wish I were standing next to him on the podium so I could have subtly whispered "normality" in his ear, just for effect. I guess I am a cynic. His face would have been priceless, though. It might have made *Time*'s cover!

Anyway, right, the benzos. Eventually black-market benzos became legally prescribed benzos. Yes, doctor, I know they are addictive. No, I will not take more than prescribed. What is the lethal dose? I mean, is it really supposed to snow tonight? Wow, I thought they said a mild winter. Goddamn *Farmer's Almanac*.

Again, don't judge. I did what was necessary to make it to where I am today (proud of where I am, or not). Of course he started with Xanax, the fast-acting God of the anxiety-ridden world. A few days later, I "cleverly" wondered where all of my thirty pills had gone?! Doc, it must not have been strong enough. No, sir, no history of drug abuse. I agree, the 0.5 milligrams was too weak. One milligram? Actually sir, why don't we move up to a full two, and I can break them in half if need be. I know, sir, I will be careful. Drinking? No, I would never drink on them.

I woke up a few days later; spilled pills and whiskey littering my dorm like a crack house. Was this what I had reduced myself to? Okay fine, pick up the pills and the pieces and take the pills like the doctor told you to. Fifteen minutes later I am out and about, ready to take on the world. And again in an hour. And again the hour after that. And after that. And again.

I don't think the Xanax is helping, sir. Yes, of course, the bottle is at home, I have a bunch left. No, sir I have never taken Valium before, does it work better? More sedating? That's okay I have a high tolerance to medicine, and I only walk to class so no "operating heavy machinery" for me. Actually, there is one more thing, I fell down the stairs and my back is really bothering me...

My writing got better; I can at least say that for myself. That is, however, the only thing in retrospect that did. I was losing weight I did not have to lose, by any means. My formerly somewhat-toned figure was atrophied. I was an AIDs patient without death to look forward to. My roommates had caught on, of course, to the extent that a few mostly-drunk sex-crazed self-centered college boys can. That extent being “yo, bro, can I get one of those?”. My response made me feel like Morpheus from the Matrix: the red pill or the blue pill. One will take you down the rabbit hole, Alice, the other, well, the other you wake up where you wake up. If you wake up, hurry up, you’re late.

I’ll tell you what; I never could understand the draw to cocaine. Sure, I tried it; let’s face it, who hasn’t. It gave me an anxiety attack, so why do something that makes you feel worse? Gimme a blunt and a couple of pills, and I was good to go. Weed is a plant, it comes from the earth. The pills were developed by smarter men than I. Now I am making excuses; claiming ignorance to the harm I was doing to my body. That same harm however, allowed my mind to function on, what I thought, and still kind of do (even now), a higher plane of existence (no pun intended) than it otherwise would have.

As you could probably have predicted, college ended up being a wash. I failed with straight A’s. I still suspect to this day that the “goodbye” speech I gave to my roommates sounded much more heartfelt than it was. I didn’t care, really. I had published here and there, and was ready to go out and face the literary world. I sold all my textbooks and came up with enough to live for a little while. I had stocked up on enough “medicine” to survive for a while, and, in my own deluded mind, I would be poet laureate by the end of the goddamn year anyway. No worries.

With school gone, there was no responsibility. I was living in the cheapest motel I could find, on nothing more than noodles and cereal. With no reason to stay sober during the day (and by sober I mean functional) my "stash" went quickly. This was problematic; I was no longer covered by the school's insurance, and the financial aid bills were soon to come. I could not afford a doctor's visit. The faster my little blue babies dwindled, the faster my mind raced. I was desperate for a solution, and I continually racked my brain. Finally, the day came. With nothing more than a few pills remaining, and fifteen dollars to my name, I decided to go out with a bang. Whiskey and benzos mix well with an opiate or two, especially if suicide is on the mind.

I had not eaten for days at this point. I assumed this would perpetuate my plan to finality. The last thing I truly remember is walking into the liquor store, picking up the cheapest bottle of whiskey I could find and stumbling (I am relatively sure at this point that I had already downed the pills) over to the register. I know he asked me for my identification; I was not yet twenty-one. This, I suppose, is what set off my chain-reaction; it was Billy Hartman all over again.

I woke up in an alley, behind a dumpster with the stench of rot overwhelming. I had no idea how long I had been there. My clothes, dingy and destroyed, were covered in a red substance I feared was blood. My first reaction, in the fog of my comedown, was that I had been mugged for my drugs. But wait, I didn't have any drugs left; I took them. What the fuck was going on?

I stumbled onto the main road. I had no idea where life was taking me, but the dream was quickly turning into a nightmare. Everyone was staring at me; look there, he is the famous writer! Let's kill him. Let's shoot him in the stomach and cut both his wrists and drag him around so everyone can see, like Brad Pitt did in *Troy*! Everywhere I went people were whispering, conspiring against me. They wanted to steal my writing; that was it. It had to be that.

Looking over my shoulder, I stumbled over to a newspaper stand. I saw a headline about a terrible murder that had been committed a few days earlier. It meant nothing to me.

I was hungry, terribly hungry. But I had no money...or did I? I was certain I had spent my last few dollars on that whiskey, but there it was in my back pocket: it was clearly the same wrinkled ten-dollar bill, and the five with the writing on the backside. I was unconcerned.

There was a drug store across the street. I stumbled in and picked up the essentials: a bottle of Excedrin, a bottle of water, and a bag of beef jerky. I went to the back of the store to pay at the pharmacy counter; it was always much less crowded. The next few minutes define my life.

The woman in front of me was picking up her prescriptions, presumably on her lunch break. Her name was Rita. Rita Henderson. That name haunts me to this day.

As I walked up behind her, she was speaking to the pharmacist. I glanced at the counter, innocently enough (?). I saw it; the bag she had been given had a chemical name on it, a generic name for the medicine she was picking up: *Diazepam 10mg tablets*. Rita Henderson.

My mind was not functioning. The chemical aspects of the brain bond to trauma much better than positive reinforcement; it is simply elemental Darwinian philosophy with Freud's superego; survival of the fittest and unconsciousness. A human will do whatever it has to do to get what its brain thinks it needs. And, at the time, my brain needed *Diazepam 10mg tablets*, much better known as Valium.

I told her to give them to me. I really did. She had a way out. In her defense, she didn't know about Billy Hartman.

She said no. I responded with one phrase before I stabbed her in the neck with the pair of scissors that were conveniently lying on the counter:

Lovely Rita, meter maid.

Lovely Rita was dead before she made it to the hospital, dead from loss of blood caused by a brutal stab wound to the neck, severing the carotid artery. I never made it out of the pharmacy.

The lights are bright, actually abnormally bright, in interrogation rooms. I suppose they do this for intimidation purposes. Either way, coming off benzos gives you a migraine as it is, or, in this day and age, the officers actually DON'T give you a cigarette. Needless to say, bright lights and migraines are not a very appealing combination. I just wanted out.

What do you want? A confession? Whatever, I waive my right for a lawyer. You don't need one? Then why…? Wait, what? This is not about lovely Rita? They didn't like when I called her that. I kept doing it.

The routine was actually quite humorous. One detective in front, slapping the table hard with crime scene photos, while the other one attacks with questions from the side. Fucking *Law and Order*! My mind drifted to that part in *Jurassic Park* (the original one) when they are explaining how raptors hunt in packs. *Clever girl*, the guy said, before being mauled to death from the side.

The detective in front was a large black man in a blue button-down, his tie loosened. He looked quite disheveled, and the tan mark on his left ring finger said recently divorced. The one to my left, the *clever girl*, so to speak, was dressed in a mildly-dressy blazer with khakis on. He actually wore aviator sunglasses. He really did. I stifled a laugh.

The black man said nothing, but simply pushed the photos toward me, while the textbook cop grilled me from the side. I ignored the photos, and told the Horatio Caine wanna-be to calm down. If I was going in for twenty-five to life, I may as well have some fun before it's over. I stopped being a smart-ass when my eyes glanced over the pictures.

The pictures, in all of their gory detail, showed a liquor store clerk badly beaten. The broken whiskey bottle next to the body left a gash in his head that presumably resulted in the massive amounts of blood that surrounded. I, I mean the assailant, had not stopped there. It appeared that his mouth had been stomped in, and his teeth littered the floor, his gold fillings glinting in the flash of the camera that had captured the image. The man had no pants on, and was lying on his side. Something was only just visible in the side of the frame. It only took one look at the subsequent picture to see what that something was: a bottle had been shoved up his rectum.

My mind flooded with thoughts of empty prescription bottles and empty whiskey bottles, waking up from comas, Billy Hartman, and of course lovely Rita.

I asked to be charged with a capital crime and put to death. The judge said he would proceed, pending a psychiatric evaluation given the heinous nature of the crimes committed.

I have always been a Democrat, really. I consider myself to be a pretty left-wing liberal, bordering socialist. As a general rule, people of this mindset are against the death penalty. It is interesting to see how perspective is simply situational. I knew it was over for me, I knew there was no going back. My mind had broken. Nature or nurture, who the fuck knows, who the fuck cares? really, at this point. I deserved to die, and I wanted to give the government the chance to make the right decision. I did, really.

I did something at that psychiatric evaluation I had not done since Billy Hartman, I faked it. I pretended. I needed them to clear me, needed them to see that I did not belong in a mental institution, but in the seventh circle of Hell. I was probably born an angel, like Lucifer, but I would fall like him as well. I was prepared to do something I had never done before, face the consequences of my actions.

Was this sobriety?

The fucking justice system did what it does best, made the wrong decision. The only thing I could possibly think as the judge stated that I was unfit to die was how many innocent people have sat exactly where I was sitting, and been told that they *would* die. Before DNA evidence, how many black men were lynched for raping the token white girl (when it was her Daddy or Uncle all the while)? And now, I of all people, ME, who murdered two different innocent people in one week, *in a drug-induced cold blooded frenzy,* was unfit to die. I was a dreg of society, and they were reading my mind like fucking tea-leaves, looking for an answer futile from the start.

And now I am writing this from a padded-room, on suicide watch, with a fucking crayon. They are pumping me with more drugs than I was on before I had two murders on my conscience, and I am just as sedated as I otherwise would have been on the outside.

I now figured out what this place is, and hospital is certainly nowhere near the word I am thinking of. This place, with the padded rooms and lack of mirrors and no FUCKING pens and regimented EVERYTHING and MANAGED medication and a MINIMAL cigarette is a fucking hospice for the mentally handicapped. They send us here to die.

This, I believe, brings us full circle once more. The beginning of life and of clarity is now. The beginning of the end so to speak because, what I have realized, is the beginning *is* the end. I have never been able to tie very good knots, and, believe me; it was not easy convincing the guards and Nurse Ratched to give me an extra sheet. But I'm so cold. Please. It's easy to pretend, like I said.

The harder part was finding a place to hang the sheet from. They seem to think of everything, don't they? However, draped over the bathroom door and tied to the handle on one end, a sheet can make a pretty effective noose.

Then there was the issue of getting the music. It all had to be right, you see? Control, it is all about control. And control, of course, is what I am taking. I gave the judge a chance, but now, now it is on my terms. I eventually persuaded one of the orderlies to let me borrow his old-school Walkman for the night, complete with *Sgt. Pepper's Lonely Hearts Club Band*. It helps me sleep, I said, brings back good memories. Oh look, one more song to go.

So this is it, I suppose. My story is over. You know what's funny? I can't seem to remember the name of the store clerk, a clear result of the lithium. I can remember one name though, as I am sliding the sheet-noose around my neck. And, we're off. For the record, April 20th, 2007. Time of death, 10:24 pm. From your nearest psych ward, this is Jim signing off!

Lovely Rita, meter maid…

What to say to simple suicide?
It is silent and sly suicide,

unwinding and binding suicide,
spring-shower suicide
hour after hour, suicide.

    Is it selfish suicide,
    or selfless homicide?

Is he still dead if nobody cries?
    Did anyone tear or cry
    when Lucifer fell from the sky?

Dark- 5

The Married Mind

The mistress mind—
the mind relied on to make decisions
"married minds" cannot make.

The glance into the "self-image mirror"
reminds of the other side,
        the not-so-kind side;
having no problem providing
        disservice and disaster.

Pragmatism provides excuses for reclusive
        Mr. Hyde's inside Dr. Whatevers everywhere.

The scare remains in removing the symbol;
        humbly harvesting your mistress
        does not hurt or burn,
but cultivate.

When your eyes lose the glint,
the sign of life, and of soul,
the ring is off your finger

and she has seduced you again,
        blinded in arrogance.

Symmetry and Monotony

I think I redefine my mind
with every objective pursued…

The objectives too subjective;
        out of control, and raging relatively rampant.

Certainly, I can control that which I understand,

        which is why I am
        where I am,

        trains of thought
        quickly collide
        without conductors,
self-made self destruction—

arrogance and self-confidence
        can be synonymous—

Alone and helpless.
        And alone.

The Norm

The stomach dropping rush;
    vulnerability is semi-consciously addicting;
    doubling-down, luck down,
    drowning in debt but knowing,
    deep inside, this time was different,

the walk away would be spectacular event,
a jovial stroll of accomplishment,

rather than a redefining and unrewarding,
    dragging and drawling,
    crawl back to empty bed-sheets.

As usual.

Its Always Blackjack

Read my lips through my eyes
        if you are blind,
realize the spatial energy
inside my mind,

break contact with God's gaze
in the outer space
        he never explained, or ignorance remains.

Be stranded,
        abandoned,
certainly out of fashion.

Cash in or cash out,
screams the dealer;

        flashbulbs fling light,
        blinding and binding to the spot,
        invisible from above.

Kindness dies behind my eyes—
see past the surface, look!
        the depths of my winter soul
        blizzard-blinded and snowbound,
        waiting to victimize.
I hate it.

The Same Game

When you run hard and swift
and trip, hitting the ground soundly
        your body is a pounding package of pain,
will you get up or give up?

Ruptured spleens or broken legs
break your stride and tear you inside,
outside, left or right,

will you choose to fight and make it right,
        or give up;

heart pounding pain and torrential rainstorms
plague potential growth, vague images of grandeur—

        deep debilitating depression
        is concession to easy demands
        of brain band-aids
        and temporary solutions
        to permanent pollution.

Will you give up and watch from the sidelines,
following guidelines of others restrictions
        and prescriptions—
feeling better but never getting better.
Find freedom (its naturally occurring).

12:56pm, 4/18/11

Failing means waking up in the wrong Hell—
tolling bells wont toll but bells will ring
out to lifeless and soul-less former people
for medicine and meals,
nicotine and coffee...

medicine and meals and nicotine
and terrible fucking coffee
until you lose it and rip your fake fucking leg off
put it through a window to escape...
what were you gonna do asshole, jump from 40 feet up?
that's not suicide or escape...simple stupidity...

so I did push-ups but I won't this time...
not this time I'll fucking die before
they lock me up, a caged animal
in a zoo they are afraid to feed...

so they tranquilize instead and I won't
I won't I won't I won't I won't
go back ever...

Meaning two things;
I get a hold on myself,
or I don't fail.

My S Poem

Falling in cracks
can swallow and consume you,
absorbing living skeletons
and masked marauders in peril…

being unmasked would be tragic, really,
stark staring
stark silent staring
and stark stupid.

Push the grind and beat the pavement
to the beats your shoes produce—
comedy down below.

Unmasked, hiding isn't optional.
Drop it.

Alone

Alone again,
puppy-dogged Sarah McGlocklin commercial,
pathetic slave.

Desire and destruction
function frequently with symbiotic AM
frequency, clarity, and disparity

disparaging my otherwise deranged
sense of senseless self-loathing—
floating high,
cloud-misted and soaring,
enjoying adrenaline again

until both chutes fail
and stark, harsh reality
slaps the ego off my smug,
overly introspective face.

Clouded, again.
Enclosing, again.
Masked, again.

Skepticism

Feeling out of place,
comfortably aware,
uncomfortably disassociated,
is going case for case
        with Cochrane, glove or not.

Perhaps your perception has changed,
rearranged with self-awareness,
        and you were always
        the same, stained picture
        in a gaudy, cheap, garage-sale frame.

Blame skepticism alone
        dethroned and bone-dry,

a stranger hitch-hiking in the desert,
contrasted clearly against city lights
        left behind.

Flashbacks...

Flashbacks are recurring rashes—
deadly diseases
capable of plague punishment...

Past—
provocation made me defensive,
defenseless against my mind
energized for too long
the rabbit lost charge.
The mirror shows black, empty
and uncaring eyes intent on destruction.

Present—
the approach becomes harder by hour
aging to vinegar,
spoiling a fine Merlot,
stamped '88.

Bitter, basic vinegar beats beautification—
paint over rust.
I'll oxidize.

Future—
I'll oxidize.
Acceptance over compromise.
Swallow before you chew.
Wheezy, winded thrusts
wait for the ball to drop.

Happy New Problem!
Sad, new day.
Day by day.

Numb- 6

(In Retrospect, the Rock Won—
I did destroy my right leg for 6 months…
However, I did jump the river, and I wrote this
book…the bright side?)

Bright afternoon anticipation,
pumped with testosterone,
trained my mind to fall in line—

follow the leader over seven feet of river,
and I had clearance…
idiotic actions actually
contain consequence.

My right foot sat calmly swaying,
knee-independent,
pointing ninety-degrees spiral.

A follower with a destroyed right leg.
Ahh, hindsight.

Mistakes and Mishaps

Forgetting to feel,
confusion—

almost an illusion, of sorts,
eluding imminence,
and undoubtedly cowardly,

defense is safer by far;
safer than a faster disaster
plastered against cast-iron
foreheads,

worn and war-torn;
still maimed and scarred,
forever marked by mistakes
and mishap,

unforgettable, and forever haunting and daunting
if not the conscious than the subconscious,
but there, always there, ready to destroy
dainty days and nifty nights,

a predator preparing to pounce
on any ounce of self still remaining.

A harsh reminder of pain.

Ignorance (Truth?)

Other's ignorance
    reflecting mood,
    deflecting face...
Disrespect, or ignorance?

Awareness of ignorance
    with a will to fight
is ignorance in and of itself

because ignorance is as ignorance does.

If I am a drug addict
    and not a post-surgical
    infected, beaten, and suffering
    patient lying in a hospital bed
    for days on end,
you must be a Registered Retard right?

Parting, she saw addict...
    I saw ignorance.

Ignorance, right
    or wrong.

Enchanted (To Poe)

Indecision is the heart,
reality runs the mind—

reality!
indifferent and unwanted,
we numb our minds when we can,
twice a day or as needed…
            as needed is vague,
            compromising in ways;

I will pay for being compromised;
I perpetually pay for chemical assistance,
in the end.

It's hard to understand, sometimes—
            life seems cyclical, a bicycle ride ruined
            by four lefts.

Thinking there *is* a difference, and *believing* difference—
            user and abuser,
            managed and prescribed…
            makes the difference…

I hope like Hell…
the spell, the spell, the spell, the spell
THE FUCKING SPELL OF ADDICTION.

Here We Go Again

Over worn and stained,
        crisp, fresh closet-stained garments
        litter my clothes-line...

Showing face to myself amounts
or compounds to some progress—
        progress for the sake of progress, and tidal in fashion.

Sometimes predictable and rational;
        volatile, yet evolving...

Mostly out of reach or touch
        in rip-tide death,
        accepting unchangeables
        and riding waves for the sake
        of breaking monotony.

Even structure would suffice
as a life-raft,
        hustling and struggling to tread water is rather tiring.

Prescription perspectives pervade,
        parade-marching
        and goose-stepping
        in one ear,
and nothing more.

Compulsive Loss

Understanding slavery as I do,
compulsion propels forward,
chest first and head deep
in potential, and redirection
of possibly accidental substance solutions.

The problem remains intact
direct and abstract—
procrastination for classless
undeserving remarks
and snappy, irrelevant retorts.

I cry for addiction prescription pads
abused and confusing
the patiently waiting patient
reading "as needed".

The patient patient patiently proceeds to numb
until the line is crossed,
because they feel so fucking good.

Confusion reduces rigorous progression
of emotional, and now unreachable
sections of the cranium
until adrenaline turns to regression.
A bottomless well, or another lesson learned.
Fuck me.

Alright, It's Oxycodone

You must erase some memories
        hiding many more…
before their consummation
becomes your deconstruction
        every time they are touched—

Tenderly stimulated or otherwise aroused,
rest assured living past lives
        delves into death-dreams
seeming more nightmarish and Devil-drawn,
every dawn,
        waking up to a case
        of mistaken monotony
        and dead identity.

Is the detoxification process
progression toward regression,

        or is a circle not a fucking circle.
Irony.

Light-7

Controlling the Beast

Embrace and sanctify strange days—
          embark on journeys
          thoughtless at heart,
          but mind-loving.

The cell is small
and it's cracked concrete
walls enclose souls,
          tick mark by tick mark;

keep digging for the light.

Brute force brings immediate truths,
wrong, right, fight, flight—
          not existential truths,
          inconsequential truths;
these are obtained
by parts of the brain
you learn to claim.

Introspection resurrects
you, bide your time.

Think immediately.

Simple Mathematics

I do not remember this part of the equation—
elation can turn to sedation.

Numb for so long,
a living coma to ignore pain and fear,
I have forgotten.

I have forgotten how to cope;
forgotten how to deal with real life
filled with real problems common
to the common man.

Did I ever know, though?
Could I ever stare a problem in the face?
stall its pace beforehand,
before it broke my stride
caused calamity gradually,
sucking the life out of me—

draining me, all that is me,
forcing me to wear the mask
I wore to hide the pain I stored?

Always alone and isolated,
my friends wore lab coats
and carried blue pads;
mad, depressed, or in pain
this week or that week
I got what I needed, weak as I was.

Everything was weak though;
out-of-control emotions
out-of-control devotion
cause out-of-control explosions
I tried in vain to contain—

I could not even explain my feelings,
much less lasso them--
    a cowboy with a child's toy
    bucked by my bronco so high
    I thought I could fly.
    I was dying then, though unaware.

Now, alive, real, and aware
I am fighting to survive
    in a game I started,
    but apparently cannot win.

Irony is tyranny for the unknown;
    awaiting another explosion,
    praying its not an implosion again.

I'll let you know when I find out.

Painting and Chipping

Lives, teeming with love
lying around every dark corner
        through fragile corridors
        formerly painted the color pain

make futile primer frail,
        and chipping renewal;

each chip is a jewel of moving forward
        and moving on,
        and moving forward,

but your still a coward
        and the paint keeps chipping
        and chipping,

chipping, and you value every chip,
        stuffing your pockets with chip-jewels,
        until they are gone
and pockets overflow...

you are rich with the future,
face to face with past—

he is an angry animal,
defensive and cornered,
downtrodden and ready to strike.

Stare him in eyes defiantly,
        deny the urge to cry,
        break your glance, and he will rise, and rise;
your life, a lie.

You, an empty shell,
        living in fear, in Hell,
following the animal,
        you are slave to his command.

Command the animal,
paint chips are gold.

Embrace your past,
treasure your future.

Regret

Lonely doors
open only wide enough
to allow subconscious
conscious decisions—

these decisions made,
blackout, drunk,
adrenaline or passion,
are not ambiguous…
fictitious farce.

Fire was not invented,
it was controlled.

Actions are concrete,
and fire burns.

Regret little.

Alcohol and Outliers

Isolated and vulnerable,
dependant and alone.

Repetitive feelings—
        reminders of me hiding inside me,
        earthquakes and heart attacks,
        smacks across the face
        disguised in lace;

I can never keep pace
        two steps forward and three steps back.

I am behind the leader,
a childhood game of conformity;
        yet I remain the deformity,

        the outlier; the odd, shaken
        martini meant to be stirred all along,
not for taste or haste,

but to break the monotony of the olives they crave;
        but I cannot produce or dispute.

Things will be what they are—
        difficult and typical.

Killer Combinations

If isolation fucked
depreciation
my commodities
would be obsolete.

I'd be down,
beat out on the street,
feeding fecal flesh
off the town,

and honestly probably
strung out by some vow
broken into pieces—
all these places
these faces

make me shoot stars,
greeting old friends and time spent realizing

I was super-sizing
to compensate
for too much space…

nature, nurture
blood and torture
are players in the same game,
not excuses for negative…
just room for improvement.

Let's call it progression for the sake of ascension.

KARMP

Her speaking eyes
spoke signs of weakness,
but harder—
a diamond, perhaps...

I was enticed,
I'll admit, when my wall fell;
and years of repression
aggression and depression
depreciated,

mere memory,
and nothing more.

Without a care,
and nothing more.

Forever changed,
and nothing more.

Thoughts to feelings,
tossed and wheeling
around, thrashed
by hard wake, stormy skies surround...

Boom. Clarity.

Outrologue

Games and Gains

It is a game of want and wanted,
a childhood game—

Christmas mornings,
bright eyes, wide mouths,
fulfillment beyond
the brim of ecstasy
under a full tree.

The sad boy sits alone,
cold, uncomforted,
no wonder in his heart,
acceptance staring back
in the toy-shop window.
His ragged image
disregarded by disgruntled
Daddy and envious Mother.

The key to life—
keeping trees filled.

Love keeps trees filled,
a game of want,
and wanted.

Exploding Stars

Seeing stars roar and soar through skies,
    clouded with judgment
    are nothing more than bright lights
igniting senses, illuminating reason without purpose
    that *will* burn out if ignored.

Closed minds are open doors.
    No anticipation.

Just classless glass...
    spidered, splintered, and waiting to implode.
    Or explode.

A supernova, if you will.

Bittersweet

It's an improvement—
delusions disappeared,
        while reclusion is not adequate amusement.

Reclusion by association
        rather than disassociation is a leech clinging to my brain
        because pseudo-pacification with most relations
        is slurring speech and sucking emotional capacity
        much more rapidly than any medication or self-medication
        has ever sapped my soul before.

A self-improvement I suppose,
        bittersweet but perhaps purposeful.

Certainly opaque, but faintly outlined
        with The Fool on the Hill.

My Only Friend…

The cosmos bent on destruction,
I try to straighten the line
I walk—
my tight-rope of shame
everyone laughs at;

no safety net,
the Graceson's from
that Batman movie,

and I saw the bottom,
this time, and again,

looking just as bleak
and inviting, as ever.

I fought though,
and I will,
there is no enough.

There is what's next.

The End.

I know apologizes are not always enough...
words can burn me and you.

I try to sympathize with support,
retort and justification
devoid of judge, jury, or attorney
but simply verdict, pieces or not..

Defective is defective
and regardless of mistake
I feel I upgraded to a smart phone,
still eye-shopping Apples of Eden,
mouth-watering at the thought.

Honestly, I'll be due for another upgrade soon.
Until then, Fuck off, (you all know your guilt).
Really, fuck off in the nicest way possible.
I know I sound irresponsible.

I grew to love rain quickly
and I learned pain the hard way
so accept me or don't,
it's your mistake...

I'm just getting started remarking
so for your sake

EXPECT A FLOOD.

P.S. I Love You All.

www.ingramcontent.com/pod-product-compliance
Lightning Source LLC
Chambersburg PA
CBHW031216270326
41931CB00006B/587

* 9 7 8 1 8 4 9 9 1 7 6 7 4 *